AF269442

JAPAN

BY ALEXIS BURLING

Essential Library

An Imprint of Abdo Publishing
abdobooks.com

ABDOBOOKS.COM

Published by Abdo Publishing, a division of ABDO, PO Box 398166, Minneapolis, Minnesota 55439. Copyright © 2023 by Abdo Consulting Group, Inc. International copyrights reserved in all countries. No part of this book may be reproduced in any form without written permission from the publisher. Essential Library™ is a trademark and logo of Abdo Publishing.

Printed in the United States of America, North Mankato, Minnesota.
102022
012023

THIS BOOK CONTAINS
RECYCLED MATERIALS

Cover Photo: Sean Pavone/Shutterstock Images (Mount Fuji); Shutterstock Images (pattern)
Interior Photos: Sean Pavone/Shutterstock Images, 4–5, 9, 98; One Studio/Shutterstock Images, 7; Artanisen/Wikimedia, 8; Shutterstock Images, 12, 15, 20, 26–27, 43, 50–51, 58, 76, 82, 84, 86–87, 97; Lucas Shu/Shutterstock Images, 16–17; Peter Hermes Furian/Shutterstock Images, 18 (Japan); Web Tools/Shutterstock Images, 18 (globe); Teerasak Chinnasot/Shutterstock Images, 23; Kyodo/AP Images, 24, 49, 68, 71, 89, 90–91, 94; Ondrej Prosicky/Shutterstock Images, 29; Yasuo Inoue/Shutterstock Images, 30; Ground Picture/Shutterstock Images, 31; M. Taira/Shutterstock Images, 33; Mami Nagaoki/Yomiuri Shimbun/AP Images, 36–37; World History Archive/Alamy, 39; Everett Collection/Shutterstock Images, 41; Anastasia Osipova/Shutterstock Images, 42; North Wind Picture Archives/AP Images, 45; Bettmann/Getty Images, 47; Shuhei Yokoyama/Yomiuri Shimbun/AP Images, 52; Eugene Hoshiko/AP Images, 54; Dmitrismirnov/Wikimedia, 57; Dustin Bradford/Getty Images Sport/Getty Images, 59; MIA Studio/Shutterstock Images, 61; Photo Network/Shutterstock Images, 62–63; Roihun Matpor/Shutterstock Images, 64, 101; Kazuhiro Nogi/Getty Images Entertainment/Getty Images, 70; Yichuan Cao/Sipa USA/AP Images, 72–73; Budrul Chukrut/SOPA Images/Sipa USA/AP Images, 74; Haruka Takahashi/Yomiuri Shimbun/AP Images, 78; Chris McGrath/Getty Images News/Getty Images, 81; Koji Sasahara/AP Images, 83; Moirenc Camille/Hemis/Alamy, 96

Editor: Angela Lim
Series Designer: Maggie Villaume

Library of Congress Control Number: 2022940380

PUBLISHER'S CATALOGING-IN-PUBLICATION DATA

Names: Burling, Alexis, author.
Title: Japan / by Alexis Burling
Description: Minneapolis, Minnesota: Abdo Publishing, 2023 | Series: Essential Library of Countries | Includes online resources and index.
Identifiers: ISBN 9781532199455 (lib. bdg.) | ISBN 9781098274658 (ebook)
Subjects: LCSH: Japan--Juvenile literature. | Asia--Juvenile literature. | Japan--History--Juvenile literature. | Geography--Juvenile literature.
Classification: DDC 952--dc23

CONTENTS

A TOUR OF JAPAN

t was finally here—the trip Suki had been looking forward to all year. Just a few years ago, she and her family had taken a vacation to Tokyo, Japan's capital. She loved touring the Imperial Palace, buying souvenirs in the glitzy Ginza shopping district, and taking in the dazzling view from the observation deck at the Tokyo Skytree—the country's tallest building. Ever since they had returned to New York City, Suki had been begging her parents to take her back to Japan so she could explore more of the country and her heritage.

This time, their vacation took them outside of Tokyo. Suki and her family planned to visit sites all

In 2019, more than 10.4 million tourists visited Tokyo.

over Japan. Their vacation would involve a lot of traveling over a short period of time. But thanks to the Shinkansen, Japan's bullet train that can travel at speeds of up to 199 miles per hour (320 kmh), the long distances wouldn't be a problem.[1]

As the plane touched down at Narita International Airport near Tokyo, Suki looked out the window in excitement. She and her family grabbed their bags and filed off the plane. Before they left the bustling airport, they picked up their seven-day Japan Rail Pass—an unlimited, multiuse rail ticket available to foreign tourists—and made their way to the Narita Express train for the 70-minute trip to Shinagawa Station in Tokyo. Then, they transferred to the Hikari Shinkansen for the 2.4-hour train ride to Kyoto. On the train ride to Hikari, Suki picked out a box of sushi and a smaller box of mochi to share with her mother. By the time they arrived at their hotel in Kyoto a few hours later, everyone was exhausted. Suki fell asleep just as her head hit the pillow.

SEEING THE SITES IN KYOTO

The next morning, the alarm clock went off at 6:00 a.m. A pillow sailed across the room and landed on Suki's head. She groaned. Suki's father grinned. He wanted to start the day early before the streets got too crowded.

Twenty minutes later, Suki was dressed, and she and her parents were out the door. They stopped at the FamilyMart convenience store to pick up some coffee. They also bought snacks including *omusubi*, or rice balls, before taking the subway to Inari Station. What Suki saw when they got off the train took her breath away.

The Fushimi Inari Taisha Shrine is a sacred space still used today by people of the Shinto faith, a Japanese religion. It is just one of more than 30,000 shrines in Japan dedicated to Inari, the Shinto god of rice. But the Fushimi Inari Taisha Shrine is the largest, oldest, and most important one of them all.[3] With roots dating back to 711 CE, the shrine was attended by members of the royal court. Today, thousands of tourists and locals alike visit the shrine each year to pay their respects to Inari and find solace in the peaceful surroundings.

First, Suki and her family passed through the looming Rōmon Gate at the shrine's entrance. Toyotomi Hideyoshi, a samurai warlord and ruler of Japan in the 1500s, gifted the gate to the site in 1589. Hideyoshi had risen to power and unified Japan in 1590 after years of civil strife. Like many of the accents on the shrine's structures, the Rōmon Gate was painted orange-red, a color believed to protect against evil forces and to promote bountiful harvests.

NOT JUST A CONVENIENCE STORE

FamilyMart is Japan's second-largest convenience store chain, behind 7-Eleven. Unlike in other countries, where convenience stores are places to pick up magazines, bottled water, and packaged food, FamilyMart has more to offer. Shoppers can pay for bus fare and buy tickets to concerts or sporting events at FamilyMart. The store also sells fresh food. Some of the mouthwatering offerings include pork buns, fried chicken, sushi, and even soufflé pudding.

TOYOTOMI HIDEYOSHI

Toyotomi Hideyoshi was born on March 17, 1537 CE. He was known as one of the three great unifiers of Japan. After 120 years of political infighting and samurai sparring for the shogun title, Hideyoshi brought the country together as one.

Hideyoshi was born into a peasant family in Nakamura, Owari Province. He joined the army of the samurai warlord Oda Nobunaga and eventually became a general. As general, he conquered rival feudal warlords and rose through the ranks to become the highest leader in the land.

During Hideyoshi's reign, he accomplished many things. In 1588, he banned all Japanese citizens besides samurai from owning weapons. He reorganized the class system and mandated the divisions be set for life. He launched much-needed tax reforms. He also built many castles and restored shrines. Hideyoshi died of natural causes on September 18, 1598.

Toyotomi Hideyoshi started off as a foot soldier and was later promoted to samurai.

The Fushimi Inari Taisha Shrine attracts thousands of visitors each year. People come to pray, admire the architecture of the torii gates, and enjoy the outdoors.

Suki then led the way through the ornately decorated *honden*, or main shrine building. She especially loved the gold-tinged decorations and the many statues of foxes wearing red bibs. Many Japanese people see foxes as messengers of the gods.

At the back of the shrine, Suki's family gazed up at Mount Inari, a majestic mountain that rises 764 feet (233 m) into the air.[4] They stood at the entrance of the Senbon Torii, which means "thousands of torii gates," at the mountain's base. Two rows of towering torii gates stood in front of them. The gates include two red-orange pillars that are connected by a beam at the top. The structures symbolize the boundary between a sacred space and the human world. Suki and her parents chose the left row to make their way up the mountain.

It took Suki and her parents two hours to walk through the gates and take in all the smaller shrines along the path. When they finally made it back to the entrance, her mother took them to one of her favorite tofu shops in all of Japan—Toyouke Chaya, which was founded in 1897. In the last few decades, the humble establishment had expanded and became a famous lunch spot. After gorging themselves on a dozen tiny plates filled with tofu presented in different ways, Suki felt she would never look at tofu the same way again. Her favorite dish was *nerigoma hairi nama yuba sashimi*. The thin strips of raw tofu skin in sesame paste were the perfect accompaniment to steamed white rice and pickled vegetables.

BRIGHT LIGHTS, BIG OSAKA

After two full days in Kyoto spent looking at wares sold in bustling street markets, ducking into stationery and art shops hidden in narrow alleys, and navigating the crowded urban neighborhoods, Suki and her family were back on the Shinkansen. This time, they were headed to Osaka, a large city to the southwest full of bright lights, flashing billboards, and towering modern skyscrapers. They stopped at a restaurant to eat one of the dishes the city is known for—*okonomiyaki*, a savory pancake-style dish filled with eggs, meat or fish, and cabbage. Then they made their way to the Osaka Castle.

To Suki, the sprawling castle complex felt like a sanctuary compared to the bustling streets outside of it. The multitiered castle gleamed with gold accents. Around the main buildings, there's a 15-acre (6 ha) park with turrets, stone walls, and moats.[6] She couldn't wait to find out more about the castle's history.

The museum located inside the complex held a treasure trove of information about the castle. It was commissioned by Hideyoshi in 1583. Construction lasted three years. When it was finished, it was the largest castle in Japan. But the castle Suki and her family were visiting was not the original building.

In 1615, Tokugawa Ieyasu, a former associate of Hideyoshi, wanted to end Hideyoshi's legacy and take control of the country. Ieyasu and his army destroyed the castle. A new version was built in its place in the 1620s. In 1868, the castle was again

The Osaka Castle has five tiers and stands 180 feet (55 m) tall.

demolished during a yearlong civil war in Japan. Historians and Japanese citizens alike hope the most recent version constructed in 1931 will stand the test of time.

Looking down at the park from an observatory, Suki was amazed by all she had learned in the museum. It was one of the highlights of the trip so far. But the best discovery was yet to come.

AN ART EXTRAVAGANZA

Suki and her parents were nearing the end of their weeklong trip. But in Suki's mind, they had saved the most exciting stop for last: Naoshima. A small island located in the Seto Inland Sea, Naoshima is known all over the world for its art installations and museums.

As soon as they got off the ferry, Suki and her parents picked up a map of the island. They spent the next two days immersed in art and Japanese culture. First, they visited the Lee Ufan Museum, a semiunderground collaboration between Japanese-Korean painter and sculptor Lee Ufan and Japanese architect Tadao Ando. The building is composed of three spare rooms that are built into the ground. The rooms are connected to a triangular stone courtyard that does not have a ceiling. The museum and surrounding landscape are filled with Ufan's stone sculptures and minimalist artworks, which are set against the backdrop of Ando's serene concrete walls. The museum offers a tranquil space where nature, architecture, and art come together as one.

Next, they visited the Chichu Art Museum. Built in 2004 and also designed by Ando, the museum has works by legends such as Claude Monet, James Turrell, and Walter De Maria. Before leaving, they bought tickets for the museum's famous electronic light show that evening.

Finally, Suki and her family finished out the afternoon gazing out at *Pumpkin*—a giant, black-and-yellow polka-dot pumpkin sculpture by Japanese artist Yayoi Kusama. The sculpture is situated on a pier that juts out into the Seto Inland Sea. Suki and her parents still had a full day tomorrow of touring the smaller art installations and street art sprinkled throughout Naoshima. But the bright and beautiful art piece seemed to represent everything magical she had seen and

done on the trip. Suki was sad to leave Japan so soon, but the trip had been even better and more amazing than she had hoped. Next to the sculpture, Suki gave both of her parents a big hug and thanked them for taking her on this vacation. She was already dreaming of the next time she could visit Japan.

A MAJESTIC COUNTRY

Suki's family visited just some of the many places Japan has to offer. Japan is home to Tokyo, the world's most populous city at approximately 37.3 million people.[7] But the country also has plenty of spaces that are perfect for meditating and finding calm. The Takachiho Gorge is one example, with cliffs that stretch for 328 feet (100 m) above the shimmering, blue-green waters of the Gokase River in Miyazaki.[8]

Japan is a multifaceted country with a long history. Today, it boasts a rich culture full of delicious cuisine, prolific art, and deep spiritual influences. With a thriving economy and an

The Gokase River winds through columns of volcanic rock at the Takachiho Gorge. One of the gorge's most famous sites is the Minainotaki waterfall, which is 56 feet (17 m) high.

efficient public transit system, the country has become not only one of the top tourist destinations across the globe but also a fulfilling place to live.

GEOGRAPHY

Japan is a stunning place with many geographical areas and landforms. The country is an archipelago and is located off the eastern coast of Asia. It stretches for approximately 2,360 miles (3,800 km).[1] Japan has a total area of 145,914 square miles (377,915 sq km), which is about the size of California.[2]

The country is surrounded by bodies of water. The Sea of Japan lies to the west, the East China Sea to the southwest, the Philippine Sea to the south, the Sea of Okhotsk to the north, and the Pacific Ocean to the east. Japan's nearest neighbors on land are Russia in northeast and China, North Korea, South Korea, and Taiwan to the west and southwest.

As a nation of islands, Japan has the sixth-longest coastline of any country in the world.

MAP OF
JAPAN

KEY:

- Capital
- City
- Point of Interest

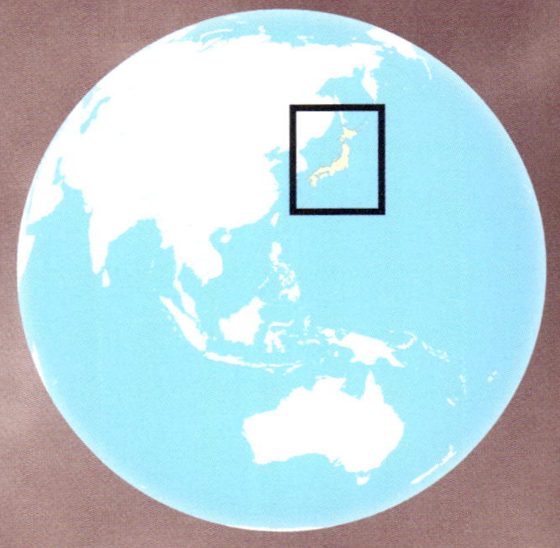

Structurally, Japan is made up of four main islands. From north to south, they are Hokkaido, Honshu, Shikoku, and Kyushu. Honshu is the largest, followed by Hokkaido, Kyushu, and Shikoku.

Many people visiting Japan for the first time think it is made up of only these four islands. But there are nearly 6,900 other smaller islands in the country.[3] The Ryukyu Islands, also called the Nansei Islands, are to the south and west of Kyushu. The Bonin Islands, which are also called the Ogasawara Islands, are another major group. There are also the Volcano Islands, otherwise known as the Kazan Islands. The Izu Islands, along with the Volcano and Bonin Islands, all lie to the south and east of Honshu. More than 400 of these small islands in Japan are inhabited.[4]

A DIVERSE LANDSCAPE

Within its borders, Japan's landscape is as diverse as it is vast. Japan sits on the Ring of Fire, a horseshoe-shaped section of the Pacific Ocean that is known for its seismic activity. The Ring of Fire lies on the intersections of tectonic plates, pieces of Earth's crust that shift and move over time.

Ninety percent of earthquakes in the world happen in the Ring of Fire. More than 450 volcanoes are located in this region too, accounting for 75 percent of the world's volcanoes.[7]

Japan's highest mountain, Mount Fuji, is just one of the country's 111 active volcanoes.[8] It reaches 12,388 feet (3,776 m) above sea level.[9] Despite its volatile nature, the site is considered sacred to many religions, including Shinto, Buddhism, and Confucianism, because of its innate beauty. Hundreds of thousands of tourists and Japanese citizens visit Mount Fuji every year.

Including its volcanoes, about two-thirds of Japan is mountainous. Forests and fields cover most of this rugged landscape. There are about 98,000 square miles (254,000 sq km) of forests and fields and about 17,000 square miles (44,000 sq km) of farmland throughout the country.[10]

Hokkaido is one of the largest wilderness areas in Japan and contains numerous national parks. It also has areas that are perfect for skiing in the winter. Its forests have several temperate thermal springs, and the landscape is sprinkled with jaw-dropping gorges. The pristine Lake Shikotsu near the city of Chitose is a caldera, or volcanic crater, that contains some of the clearest water in the world. It's also the most transparent lake in Japan. The lake is so breathtaking that the Lake Shikotsu Ice Festival is held in January and February every year to attract tourists.

As a nation of islands, Japan has a long coastline of 18,486 miles (29,751 km)—the sixth-longest coastline in the world.[11] But the country's coastal areas aren't all sandy beaches. Instead, many of

the country's oceanside spots are just as craggy as the rest of the surrounding mountain landscape. The Kitayamazaki coast, for example, is a five-mile (8 km) stretch of coastline on the northeastern tip of Honshu Island. It features cliffs that tower approximately 656 feet (200 m) above the roiling ocean water.[14]

Japan is also home to many estuaries and rivers. At 228 miles (367 km) long, the Shinano River is the country's longest river.[15] It begins in Mount Kobushi in the Japanese Alps and flows northwest through Matsumoto and Niigata before draining into the Sea of Japan. The river provides much of the water for the rice fields throughout Niigata's lower plains.

A VARIED CLIMATE

Japan is located in the Northern Hemisphere—the same as the United States and Canada. Therefore, its seasons are similar to those on the East Coast of the United States. The seasons range from subarctic in the north to subtropical in the south. Seasonal winds and ocean currents have the biggest impact on Japan's temperate marine climate.

Views of the Kitayamazaki Cliffs can be seen from observation decks in Sanriku Fukko National Park. The cliffs are nicknamed the Alps of the Sea.

During the winter, gusty Siberian winds pick up moisture from the Sea of Japan and drop it onto the Japanese Alps, causing heavy snowfall and freezing temperatures on the western sides of Hokkaido and Honshu. On the eastern side of Japan, the winter months remain cold but relatively dry. In the summer, the humid air feels thick with moisture throughout most of the country. Though temperatures vary from region to region, the average summer temperature in Japan is approximately 77 degrees Fahrenheit (25°C). The average winter temperature in the country is about 41 degrees Fahrenheit (5°C).[16]

In addition to the fluctuation in temperature, Japan also has two major rainy seasons. The first

Since 1920, temperatures in Japan have risen by more than 1.8 degrees Fahrenheit (1°C).[17]

Typhoon Chanthu made landfall on eastern and central Japan on September 18, 2021. It brought high waves and heavy rainfall.

begins in early summer, and the second occurs during the fall. Heavy thunderstorms and massive typhoons occur during the rainy seasons, especially in the southwestern part of the country. The rainiest areas in Japan receive more than 80 inches (203 cm) of annual precipitation.[18] The central-western part of Honshu Island, Kyushu's central-southern section, and Shikoku's inland and southern areas get the most rainfall per year. In contrast, the northern section of Hokkaido receives the least amount of precipitation.

According to many tourist guidebooks, the best time to visit Japan is in the spring, from early April through the middle of June. At this time of the year, the weather throughout many of the islands is temperate and dry. The average temperatures during spring are between 63 degrees Fahrenheit (17°C) in the north of the country and 81 degrees Fahrenheit (27°C) in the south.[19]

In contrast, temperatures can shoot up to above 100 degrees Fahrenheit (38°C) throughout most of the country between late June and August.[20] The skies are often cloudy, and the air feels humid and sticky. Getting caught in a downpour is also likely. Thunderstorms and typhoons can cause mudslides and floods.

Japan's heavy rainfall and storms can cause high humidity, but there are benefits to the ample precipitation. Because of the large amounts of rain Japan receives, the country is a place of diversity and beauty. It is full of lush landscapes, roaring rivers, and thriving ecosystems. Some of the most wondrous things about the country are its plants and animals.

CHAPTER THREE

PLANTS AND ANIMALS

From north to south and east to west, Japan is a country full of flora and fauna. Because of the temperate climate and heavy annual rainfall, a variety of plants and animals can thrive in Japan. According to the Convention on Biological Diversity, the country has more than 90,000 known species.[1]

Life in Japan doesn't just flourish on land. Approximately 50 of the world's 127 marine mammal species swim and reproduce in the waters surrounding the islands.[2] About 122 species of seabirds and 3,700 marine fish species call the country's seas and ocean their home too.[3]

Japan's abundant rainfall gives rise to forests that provide habitat to many kinds of animals.

According to Japan's Ministry of the Environment, there are five distinct regions in Japan where different plants and animals live. These are the northlands, mountains, rural areas, wetlands, and subtropics. Throughout these ecosystems, many species of flora and fauna coexist, sometimes in harmony and other times in direct conflict with each other.

NORTHLANDS

In Hokkaido, Japan's northernmost major island, there are many types of plants and animals that can't be found elsewhere in the country, such as hazel grouses and Siberian salamanders. Brown bears—Japan's largest land animal—also live only in the forests and mountains of Hokkaido. They have a large grazing range, sometimes hundreds of square miles.

In the winter, Steller's sea eagles and spotted seals migrate to Hokkaido from farther north. From February to April, drift ice forms off the east coast of Hokkaido, making it the perfect breeding ground for seals. Other mammals that can adapt to the northland's sometimes harsh conditions include the Sika deer, the Hokkaido red fox, the Japanese crane, and the pika, a tiny rodent-like mammal that eats moss, ferns, and mushrooms.

When the northlands aren't covered in snow, flowers that flourish in high altitudes, such as varieties of Jacob's ladder and narcissus anemone, explode in full bloom. The *Rebun-kinbai-so*, a variety

About 40 percent of Japan's land mammals, 60 percent of reptiles, and 80 percent of amphibians are native to the country.[4]

of ledebour globeflower, is a type of plant found only on Rebun Island, the northernmost island in Japan. In June, it blooms bright yellow-orange or orange-red. The Sakhalin fir and Yezo spruce trees are common throughout central to northern Hokkaido.

MOUNTAINS

Mountains extend down the spine of Japan. Depending on the latitude and altitude, different plants and animals make up the habitat. In high elevations, fir, spruce, and larch trees are prevalent. In middle-altitude zones, alpine grasslands, needle-leaved forests, deciduous broad-leaved forests, or evergreen broad-leaved forests are the dominant landscapes. Oak, maple, linden, birch, ash, elm, and walnut trees thrive in lower mountain elevations.

The golden eagle is one of the largest birds of prey in Japan, with a wingspan of more than

In Japan, red-crowned cranes are symbols of good luck and happiness.

Once threatened by overhunting and habitat loss, conservation efforts have increased the number of Japanese serow.

6.5 feet (2 m).[5] It eats hares, birds, and reptiles. Because of deforestation, the golden eagle is listed as an endangered species. The rock ptarmigan, a bird species that has survived since the Ice Age, is also facing the risk of extinction because of habitat loss and climate change. Its feathers turn from gray to white in the winter. Both the golden eagle and the rock ptarmigan live mostly in the alpine region, though the golden eagle can also frequent the lowlands when hunting for prey.

Farther down the mountains, many animal species populate the evergreen and deciduous broad-leaved forests. One example is the Japanese serow, a horned animal that looks like a cross between a goat and an antelope. The mountains are home to many birds, including the black woodpecker and the narcissus flycatcher. The narcissus flycatcher sings a melodious song to attract mates. One of the most beloved native animals in this area is the Japanese macaque. These monkeys live farther north than any known primate in the world. They have a beard of whiskers, brown fur speckled with white or gray, and wrinkled faces. Macaques are often compared to old men by people who are lucky enough to witness them in their natural habitat.

The forest floor also brims with life. The Eastern-Japanese common toad and the small Japanese field mouse are just two of the many creatures that hop and burrow among the five-finger ferns that cover the forest floor. Honey mushrooms, named for their golden colors, support the forest's ecosystem by helping decompose dead trees and fallen leaves.

RURAL AREAS

Some animals have adapted to live alongside people in Japan's rural areas. For example, some regions of the country are covered with woodlands, rice paddies, irrigation canals, and ponds. These spots are known as *satoyama*—or the

borderlands between human environments and mountain foothills—and are rife with birds, insects, and other wildlife.

The rural woodlands are full of interesting creatures, such as the giant stag beetle and the Japanese rhinoceros beetle. The male beetles of both species have large horns and jaws that are used to mark their territories and defend themselves when fighting for mates. The great purple emperor butterfly, the national butterfly of Japan, is a rare treat to see because it is endangered in some areas of the country. Males of this species have vibrant purple wings, while females tend to be duller in color. These butterflies drink tree sap. The *tanuki*, also known as a raccoon dog, is a species native to Japan that is related to wolves, foxes, and domestic dogs. They are nocturnal animals that live in the woodlands and travel in packs.

Giant water bugs are the largest aquatic insects in Japan and live among the Kanto dandelions in paddies. They eat small fish and frogs. Luciola, also known as Japanese fireflies, glow all over

Raccoon dogs are featured in Japanese folklore as trickster spirits. Legends and art depict them as mischievous shape-shifters, but later statues of raccoon dogs were considered lucky charms.

Japan in the summertime. They are attracted by clean water and live mostly in rural areas. Many Japanese people believe the fireflies' lights symbolize the souls of people who have recently died. There are viewing parties throughout the country, including the Kugayama Firefly Festival in Tokyo.

The Japanese oriental white stork and the Japanese crested ibis are gorgeous birds with long beaks and typically white plumage. They were once in danger of extinction because of the excessive use of toxic chemicals for farming in their habitats. But increased awareness and conservation programs have allowed these species to rebound.

WETLANDS

There are plenty of diverse inland environments in Japan due to the amount of rainfall the country receives each year. When the rain trickles down from the mountains and forests, it flows into the rivers, lakes, and marshes that populate the landscape and the tidal flats that line the shores. Migratory birds such as snipes, plovers, and kingfishers settle in the areas to breed.

Exquisite flowers bloom in season, including a reddish-purple orchid called the *tokisou* and the common sundew, an insectivorous plant that traps and digests insects using the brightly colored, sticky hairs on its leaves. The perennial floating water lily found in marshes from Hokkaido through Kyushu has white flowers that open in the morning and close at night.

Horseshoe crabs and loggerhead sea turtles are both endangered in Japan. Hatchling sea turtles spend 20 to 30 years in the Pacific Ocean before they mature. The Nagatahama Beach on the island of Yakushima is one of the most significant sea turtle breeding sites in the world.

According to the International Union for Conservation of Nature (IUCN) Red List of Threatened Species, 5.6 percent of plant and animal species in Japan are critically endangered.[7]

SUBTROPICS

The subtropics are some of the most scenic places in Japan. On the subtropical islands, such as Okinawa and Amami Ōshima, coral reefs and mangrove forests abound in the coastal areas. In forested regions, giant cedars—some hundreds of years old—tower over the wildlife.

Yakushima is an island in southern Japan near Hiroshima. It is home to *Cryptomeria japonica*, a cedar-like species native to the country. Some of these trees are believed to be more than 2,500 years old. The largest tree is about 83 feet (25 m) tall with a massive trunk that is nearly 17 feet (5.1 m) in diameter.[11] The ancient forest is so beautiful that it was depicted in *Princess Mononoke*, an anime movie by Japanese animator and director Hayao Miyazaki.

Off land, humpback whales sing and flap their tails as they sing. They can weigh as much as 40 short tons (36 metric tons) and grow to be 52 feet (16 m) long.[8] Okinawa is the habitat of the northernmost living dugong, an endangered marine mammal that dines on seaweed. Dugongs are prominently featured in the folklore and rituals of the Okinawan people. Because of this, these shy creatures are considered to be cultural monuments by Japanese law.

In the subtropic mountains, giant ferns and giant Sudajii trees flourish in the lush, mossy forests. Ogasawara flying foxes and crested serpent eagles dominate the air, while Amami rabbits hide from mongooses on the forest floor. Mongooses were introduced into the area to keep the snake population down. However, they preyed on the Amami rabbit instead, pushing the rabbits to the brink of extinction.

The Ogasawara Islands are 620 miles (1,000 km) south of Tokyo.[9] Many of these islands are extremely isolated, with very little human presence. The Ogasawara Islands are covered in subtropical forests. More than 100 recorded native land snail species and 195 bird species live there.[10]

CHAPTER FOUR

HISTORY

Today Japan is an archipelago, but the nation wasn't always made of islands. It was once connected to mainland Asia, allowing the first humans to inhabit Japan. They migrated from mainland Asia around 10,000 BCE.

The first recorded period in Japanese history was known as the Jōmon period (10,500–300 BCE). People lived in permanent housing for the first time. They made homes out of stones with clay roof structures or lived in pit dwellings. Around 300 BCE, the Yayoi, another group of peoples from mainland Asia, sailed from parts of China and the Korean peninsula to settle in Japan. This time was called the Yayoi period (300 BCE–300 CE). The Yayoi introduced agriculture to the region and began cultivating rice. The Yayoi lived

The Jidai Matsuri Festival is celebrated annually in Kyoto. Parade participants dress in historically accurate costumes from the past 1,100 years.

in small farming villages and formed the first local political clans in Japan.

Japan has its origins as a monarchal nation. The monarchy may have been created by Emperor Jimmu around 660 BCE. Jimmu is a legendary figure who came to power after warring with local clans. He and his followers formed the imperial dynasty, and Japan has had an emperor ever since.

Jimmu, Japan's first emperor, is believed to have come to power in 660 BCE. Most scholars agree that the start of Japan's first monarchy is based on myth. Part of the legend states that Emperor Jimmu was the great-great-grandson of the sun goddess Amaterasu. The story goes that he laid claim to his throne by conquering a local clan with the help of a golden bird.

ANCIENT AND MEDIEVAL JAPAN

Japan's domain continued to grow. By 710 CE, an emperor ruled over the land. The first taxes were collected at this time. *Shōen*, types of estates, were owned by powerful families, court aristocrats, or religious institutions. Peasants maintained the land and managed the households of the ruling elite. That year, the first imperial capital was built at Heijō-kyō, present-day Nara. The capital city was moved to Nagaoka in 784. In 794, the capital moved to Heian-kyō, which is now Kyoto, where it stayed for more than 1,000 years. Each time the capital moved, Japan experienced political reform.

At the start of the Medieval Japan period (1185–1503), the emperor's power declined, and the position became more symbolic. The power had shifted to a military warlord called a shogun,

Samurai were skilled swordsmen who wore intricately detailed armor. Swords were important to these soldiers because a man's honor was said to live in his sword.

who governed a feudal society. In feudal societies, areas of land are owned by lords, called daimyo in Japan. The shogun appointed daimyo, and the daimyo hired samurai to protect their lands. Though the shogun held the ultimate authority in the land, the central government was relatively weak during the medieval period. Daimyo attempted to gain more land and power, ordering their samurai to fight with samurai employed by rival lords. For more than 800 years, daimyo and samurai clashed in a series of civil wars as the shogun worked to reestablish control over

the country. The shogun title was passed down through a family line. However, the shogunate collapsed several times during the medieval period, and shoguns from different families rose to power.

Minamoto Yoritomo was the first shogun of Japan. His government was the Kamakura shogunate (1185–1333). During the Kamakura shogunate, Mongolian forces tried to invade Japan, sailing toward Kyushu in 1274 and again in 1281. Samurai defended the island, and each side suffered heavy losses. The Mongols retreated both times. Some scholars believe that typhoons played a role in the retreats, with strong storms destroying much of the Mongolian navy.

Another major conflict erupted during the Ashikaga shogunate (1336–1573). The Ōnin Civil War (1467–1477) broke out near Kyoto because of a dispute over shogun successions. This struggle for power marked the beginning of the Warring States period. Daimyo battled over who would claim the title of shogun. Kyoto was ravaged in the process.

In 1543, during the Warring States period, the Portuguese arrived in Japan after their ship was blown off course by a typhoon. They became the first Europeans in Japan. The Japanese at first saw the Portuguese as *nanban*, or southern barbarians. But Japan began to trade with Portugal, importing tin, gold, and silk and exporting swords, lacquerware, and silver. The Portuguese— and later the Spanish—brought Christianity to Japan and began converting the Japanese to the religion.

In 1590, Toyotomi Hideyoshi unified the daimyo of Japan, leading to the end of the Warring States period. At this time, there were approximately 215,000 Japanese Christians.[1]

Some Japanese art depicts Portuguese traders and fashion.

Hideyoshi became worried about the growing European and religious influences in the country. In order to protect his power, Hideyoshi issued a decree expelling all Christians from Japan. However, this decree was not enforced well during Hideyoshi's rule.

THE EDO PERIOD

The Warring States period did not officially end until 1603, when the Tokugawa shogunate was formed. Tokugawa Ieyasu was the first shogun of the Edo period (1603–1867). The Tokugawa family reigned in Japan for more than 200 years. After hundreds of years of strife during Japan's medieval period, the Edo period is viewed by historians as a time of religious, political, and social order.

In 1639, the Tokugawa shogunate adopted the *sakoku*, or closed-country, policy. This was a series of restrictive measures that aimed to remove European and religious influences from Japan. Japanese people were not allowed to leave the country, and trade with other nations was strictly limited. Sakoku outlawed trade with any

CHRISTIANITY IN JAPAN

In 1597, Hideyoshi executed 20 Christians and six foreign officials as an example of his stance toward Christianity.[2] In the years that followed, the Tokugawa shogunate also worked to limit the religion. The Japanese government banned Christianity and began destroying Christian churches. In 1637, people living on the Shimabara Peninsula rebelled, protesting against high taxes. Many of the people involved were Christians. The Japanese government stopped the rebellion and became stricter in its efforts to eliminate Christianity from Japan. The government killed an estimated 2,000 Christians who refused to give up their faith.[3] Practicing Christianity in Japan was legalized in 1873.

Western nation aside from the Netherlands. It also prohibited Japanese merchants from exporting their goods abroad except to China and Korea.

The Japanese economy flourished. Rice, sesame oil, sugarcane, mulberry, tobacco, and cotton crops boomed. Japan's manufacturing industry grew, as did the size of Japanese cities. Edo, Kyoto, and Osaka became cultural hubs. New art forms exploded in popularity, such as kabuki theater and woodblock printing. Kabuki theater includes singing and dancing in lavish costumes.

On July 8, 1853, US Navy commodore Matthew Perry sailed to Edo with four warships. He demanded that Japan reestablish trade with Western nations. Reopening Japan would give the United States a port in the Pacific Ocean, which would have economic and military benefits. He returned the next year with

Kabuki theater, which started in the early 1600s, is still performed in Japan today.

more warships to further pressure Japan. Unable to withstand an attack, the country was forced to accept the US terms. The United States and European nations soon began to trade with Japan, bringing an end to the Edo period.

THE MEIJI PERIOD

In 1867, the Tokugawa shogunate fell. As a result, major changes took place all over Japan. The Meiji Constitution of 1889 transitioned Japan into a nation-state, and the emperor regained sovereign power. Emperor Meiji, who was just 14 years old at the time, became the head of state. The feudal structure of Japan gradually broke down. Former feudal lords had to return their land to the emperor. The country was restructured into districts called prefectures. A parliamentary government system was also adopted. It consisted of a legislature with a lower and upper house, a prime minister, and a cabinet.

Japan's military became stronger and more active due to trade with Western nations. Meanwhile, China's military was weakened by wars with European countries. Japan saw this as an opportunity to seize Korea, which had been under China's control for many years. This led to the First Sino-Japanese War (1894–1895) with China. Japan easily defeated China, and Chinese troops were forced to retreat. Japan and China signed the Treaty of Shimonoseki, which officially ended the war. The treaty gave Japan control of Korea and other territories, including the Liaodong Peninsula. Russia, France, and Germany feared the growing strength of Japan and intervened. They forced Japan to give control of the Liaodong Peninsula to Russia.

Japan's victory in the First Sino-Japanese War was due in part to its use of modern warships and technology.

The loss of the Liaodong Peninsula to Russia increased hostilities between the two nations, eventually leading to the Russo-Japanese War (1904–1905). Japan ambushed Port Arthur, a Russian port, and the war raged for a year in Korea and the Sea of Japan. Both sides experienced significant casualties, but Japan emerged victorious. This marked the first time an Asian nation had defeated

a European power in modern times. As a result of the war, Japan gained total control of Korea, which remained under Japanese authority until 1945.

TWENTIETH CENTURY AND BEYOND

Japan entered World War I (1914–1918) on August 23, 1914. The country declared war on Germany, joining the United Kingdom, France, Russia, and several smaller nations as Allied powers. China attempted to join the Allies, but Japan did not allow China to join so that Japan could remain the dominant power in Asia.

One of the reasons Japan sided with the Allies was because it sought to gain control of German-held territories, including Qingdao. Located on China's Shandong Peninsula, Qingdao was one of Germany's largest overseas naval bases. Japanese troops successfully took over the base by the end of 1914. The following year, Japan used its involvement in the war to force China to agree to its Twenty-one Demands. This document required China to surrender control of Chinese territory as part of Japan's wartime needs.

JAPAN'S TREATMENT OF KOREA

From 1910 to 1945, Japan implemented harsh rules in Korea to exercise control over the country. The Japanese government outlawed speaking Korean in all schools and universities. It burned more than 200,000 Korean historical documents and prohibited teaching history from texts that were not approved by the Japanese government.[4] During World War II until the end of the Japanese occupation in Korea, the Japanese forced hundreds of thousands of Korean women into prostitution.

Tensions between Japan and China escalated following World War I. In 1931, Japan invaded and occupied Manchuria. Japan launched a major invasion of China as part of the Second Sino-Japanese War (1937–1945). Japan captured major cities and used tactics that other nations criticized during the conflict. For example, Japan captured Nanking in December 1937. According to historians, Japanese troops massacred an estimated 300,000 Chinese civilians and raped 80,000 Chinese women in the Nanking area.[5]

By 1940, neither Japan nor China had claimed victory in the war. Japan entered World War II (1939–1945) in September of that year, joining with Germany and Italy to form the Axis powers. Economic sanctions placed on Japan by Western countries such as the United States added to the country's hostility. In response to the sanctions, Japan bombed Pearl Harbor, a US naval base on the coast of Honolulu, Hawaii,

Japanese soldiers entered Nanking during the Second Sino-Japanese War.

on December 7, 1941. More than 2,400 Americans died in the attack.[6] These actions prompted the United States to enter World War II.

Following the bombing of Pearl Harbor, Japan advanced throughout Asia, occupying the Dutch East Indies, British Singapore, New Guinea, and the Philippines. But by 1944, the Allies—which included the United States, the United Kingdom, and Russia—started claiming more victories. Still, Japan refused to back down. In August 1945, the United States dropped atomic bombs on two Japanese cities: Hiroshima and Nagasaki. Hiroshima was an important military base, and Nagasaki was a major port city. The bombings instantly killed more than 130,000 Japanese civilians.[7] On August 15, 1945, Emperor Michinomiya Hirohito announced Japan's surrender.

As part of Japan's unconditional surrender in World War II, the country relinquished all the territory it had conquered since 1895. The United States began a military occupation of Japan, and the Japanese military was stripped of its arsenal. The United States drafted a new constitution for Japan in 1946 that went into effect the following year. In 1951, Japan signed a peace treaty with the United States and 47 other countries. When the treaty went into effect, Japan became an independent country again.

Japan reestablished itself as an economic powerhouse by the early 1970s. A decade later, the country had become a major leader in the global manufacturing and technology markets.

It hosted the Olympic Games twice—once in Tokyo in 1964 and again in 2021. It also hosted the 1970 World Expo in Osaka.

Today, Japan remains one of the world's global superpowers. It still has an emperor. Hironomiya Naruhito became the emperor of Japan on May 1, 2019. Naruhito was still the emperor of Japan in 2022. His reign signaled the beginning of the Reiwa period. *Reiwa* means "beautiful harmony."

CHAPTER FIVE

PEOPLE AND CULTURE

Home to beautiful pastoral areas and some of the world's largest cities, Japan is a country full of rich culture, delicious food, deep spiritual beliefs, and all types of people. In 2022, there were approximately 124.2 million people residing in Japan.[1] However, Japan's population is slowly declining because of its aging population. The percentage of its population aged 65 or older is the highest in the world. There are a record 80,000 people in Japan who are over 100 years old.[2] In 2020, approximately 36.2 million people in Japan were 65 or older.[3] This age group is projected to represent about a third of the country's population by 2036.[4]

For about two weeks in spring, cherry blossoms sweep across Japan. For centuries, people have gathered under the trees for *hanami*, or "flower viewing," festivals.

The Gion Matsuri festival is one of the biggest cultural celebrations in Japan. The Yamaboko Junkō float processions are the biggest part of the monthlong festival in Kyoto.

Japan has one of the lowest fertility rates in the world, which contributes to the country's aging population. In 2020, that figure was 1.34 children per woman.[5] Many economists attribute the low fertility rate to the fact that more Japanese women are marrying later in life. Others are postponing starting a family. Some women are deciding to forgo marriage or having children altogether. This means there aren't enough babies being born to replace the elder generation.

Japan has a relatively uniform ethnic makeup compared to some other countries. About 98 percent of people living in Japan are Japanese. Chinese people make up 0.6 percent of the population, and Koreans make up 0.4 percent.[6] The remaining part of the population includes a mix of people of other ethnic backgrounds, including Vietnamese, Filipino, and Brazilian.

LANGUAGE

Japanese is the official language of Japan, and it is the language that is most widely spoken in the country. The language has many dialects, or forms of language that are particular to a specific region or group. Speakers of one dialect don't always understand what a speaker of another dialect is saying. Almost everyone in the country speaks standard Japanese in addition to a hometown dialect.

The language has a distinctive writing system and alphabet influenced by other cultures. More than 1,500 years ago, Japanese people adopted Chinese characters for writing. These characters are called kanji and represent words or concepts. Japanese people also use an additional alphabet, called kana. Unlike the Western alphabet, where letters represent a single vowel or consonant, each kana stands for a syllable. Today, most Japanese writing is a mixture of kanji and kana.

In newspapers and magazines, Japanese is usually printed from top to bottom. The text is organized in vertical columns and runs from right to left. In some books, especially those appealing to a

In June 2022, there were about 37.2 million people living within Tokyo's larger metropolitan area. That's about 29 percent of Japan's overall population.[7]

Participants showcase their work during the 2022 Calligraphy Contest in Tokyo. Calligraphy is a decorative form of handwriting.

Western audience, the layout is slightly different. There, Japanese is printed horizontally and runs from left to right.

RELIGION

Japan is a mostly secular country. There is no dominant religion, and Japanese people often follow practices from multiple religious traditions. Most of the country is split between Shinto and Buddhism. About 48.6 percent are Shintoists and 46.3 percent are Buddhists.[8]

Shinto is the oldest religion in Japan. It can be found in records as far back as 300 BCE. The main tenet of Shinto is the worship of kami, spirits that inhabit the natural world. If honored properly, these supernatural beings infuse people's lives with benefits, such as good health and business success. Shinto shrines, or *jinja*, are the sacred homes of one or more kami. Shinto followers go to these shrines to worship and perform rituals. There are nearly 80,000 Shinto shrines scattered throughout Japan.[9] One such shrine is the Ise Grand Shrine. This shrine is dismantled every 20 years and completely rebuilt nearby to signify the Shinto belief of death and renewal. The practice is also a way of keeping artisan skills and ancient modes of architecture alive. The tradition has been going on since the 700s CE.

Buddhism is newer to Japan. It was introduced from China and Korea around 500 CE. Buddhism is a spiritual path for transcending the suffering of existence. Buddhists believe in samsara, the endless cycle of birth, death, and rebirth. The cycle is built upon karma, the tally of good and bad actions from a person's many lives. Buddhists believe that a release from this cycle is achieved only through

JAPAN'S INDIGENOUS POPULATION

The vast majority of people living in Japan are Japanese. But within that large category, there are three major subgroups. Mainland Japanese make up the largest subgroup. The Ainu peoples are Indigenous and were the earliest settlers of Hokkaido. The Ryukyuans are another group of Indigenous people who inhabit the Ryukyu archipelago, near Kyushu and Okinawa. In 1879, the Meiji government invaded and annexed both of these territories. It persecuted the Ainu and Ryukyu people. To this day, they are still dealing with the loss of their lands and the denial of their cultural and spiritual beliefs.

enlightenment. There are many sacred Buddhist temples throughout Japan's towns, cities, and villages. One of the most breathtaking is Kinkaku-ji in Kyoto. Thousands of people visit this temple each year to worship or learn more about Buddhist history. Each floor has a different style of architecture. The top two floors are covered in gold leaf.

Aside from Shinto and Buddhism, a small number of other religions are practiced in Japan. One percent of Japan's population is Christian. The remaining 4 percent is made up of followers of Islam, Baha'i, Hinduism, and Judaism.[10]

ARTS, SPORTS, AND CULTURE

As a country, Japan is known for its prolific artistic output. One of its ancient traditions is *shodō*, or "calligraphy." Brought over from China more than 1,000 years ago, the decorative handwriting comes in many forms. The most popular style of shodō is *gyosho*, which means "moving style." Gyosho represents fluidity and motion. Throughout Japanese history, shodō has been used to record haikus, a Japanese poetry form. Some of the most celebrated examples include the writings of haiku master Matsuo Bashō, who lived in the 1600s.

MATSUO BASHŌ

Matsuo Bashō was born in Ueno, Japan, in 1644. His birth name was Matsuo Kinsaku. Matsuo came from a long lineage of samurai, but he chose to do something different with his life. He got his start as a poet by learning *renga*, a form of poetry collectively written by multiple poets.

After moving to Edo in his late 20s, Bashō perfected the art of writing haikus. This form of Japanese poem consists of three lines that have a total of 17 syllables. The first and third lines each have five syllables, and the second line has seven syllables. Matsuo started publishing under the name Bashō, which is a type of tree. In 1682, he left Edo to travel throughout Japan, finding inspiration for his poetry in nature. He kept a travelogue called *The Narrow Road to the Deep North*, which was published in 1694. It brought recognition to the *haibun*, a form of writing that connects haiku and narrative prose.

Bashō was the author of many anthologies and volumes of poetry. Some include *Monkey's Raincoat* and *The Seashell Game*. Bashō died in Osaka on November 28, 1694.

Bashō is known as one of the most famous Japanese poets that has ever lived.

Ikebana, the art of flower arranging, and ukiyo-e, the art of creating woodblock prints, are two other long-standing Japanese artistic traditions. Ukiyo-e became a popular art form during the Edo period as a way to illustrate the everyday life of people living in Kyoto. Some woodblock prints depicted pastoral scenes, while others featured sumo wrestlers or elegant portraits of geisha.

Modern ukiyo-e artists apprentice with an expert, and the art form is rarer now than it was in the past. But other visual art forms continue to flourish in ukiyo-e's place. Origami is the art of folding paper to create decorative art, such as cranes. Japanese comic books and graphic novels called manga and Japanese animation called anime are two media that continue to attract fans around the world. Hayao Miyazaki is one of the most famous Japanese animators and film directors. His animation company, Studio Ghibli, has produced more than 20 feature films, including *Spirited Away* and *Howl's Moving Castle*.

Kabuki and Noh are traditional forms of Japanese theater that are still popular throughout the country. Noh got its roots in Japan in the 1500s. Performances were based on ancient Japanese legends and involved song and dance. Masks were worn to portray a variety of characters. Though only

THE MAGIC OF MANGA

Manga is a Japanese literary art form that resembles comic books, but it is also different in a few ways. Manga stories are read from right to left and back to front. Additionally, they are usually published in black and white, not color. In 2020, annual sales of manga books and magazines in Japan reached more than $4.5 billion.[11]

Los Angeles Angels pitcher and slugger Shohei Ohtani first played professional baseball in Japan. He played in the MLB All-Star game in 2021.

men were allowed to perform in Noh theater traditionally, a growing number of women have been permitted to do so since the 1900s.

Baseball is Japan's most popular sport. It was first introduced to the country in 1872. The highest level of the game is Nippon Professional Baseball, which includes two leagues, the Central League and the Pacific League. Other favored sports in Japan include sumo wrestling, soccer, golf, karate, and other forms of martial arts.

Fashion is also huge in Japan. Wardrobe choices range from *wafuku*, a style of traditional Japanese clothing, to *yōfuku*, Western-style attire. The *furisode* is a kimono that is worn only by

unmarried women. *Tabi*, or split-toed socks, are worn with *geta*, wooden sandals. *Kawaii* is a modern trend that's become especially popular with single girls. From flouncy dresses, big bows, and bubblegum-colored skirts, kawaii styles emphasize looking young and cute.

A typical kaiseki meal can cost more than 30,000 Japanese yen (more than $220 in US dollars) per person, not including drinks.[12]

FOOD AND DRINK

Japanese food is renowned for being a simple yet refined cuisine. From meals prepared by celebrated chefs, such as sushi master Jiro Ono, to dishes served in back-alley mom-and-pop bars in Osaka and Kyoto, there are plenty of culinary delights in Japan. Perhaps the most well-known dishes are sushi and sashimi, which involve thin, artfully prepared slices of seafood or vegetables eaten at room temperature. While sashimi is served on its own, sushi is rice that often serves as a base with seafood or other ingredients and sauces on top. Sushi rice can also be served as a roll. At *kaitenzushi* restaurants, small plates of sushi are delivered to diners on a conveyor belt.

Unlike in some countries where meat, fish, and chicken are served at almost every meal, vegetarian dishes are widely available throughout Japan. A fermented bean called natto and products made from soy, including tofu and miso, are seen on many Japanese menus. Noodles, such as soba, ramen, and udon, are especially popular in soups. Some soups are made without meat while others, like *tonkotsu* ramen, are prepared with pork.

To finish off the meal, mochi—gooey rice balls which may be filled with sweet red bean paste—are a favorite treat of Japanese kids. For adults, sake (pronounced SAW-kay)—an alcoholic drink that is made by fermenting rice—is served either hot or cold. A nonalcoholic beverage called matcha is a soothing end to any dining experience. It's made from finely ground green tea leaves and is especially popular in Japanese tea ceremonies. Kaiseki is the most exclusive experience of all. It consists of a set menu chosen by the chef to highlight in-season ingredients. There are usually seven to 14 courses.

CHAPTER SIX

POLITICS

The current Japanese government dates back to the end of World War II, when the country lost to the Allied powers. The United States occupied Japan and forced it to adopt a new constitution. The constitution, which was written by the US government, went into effect on May 3, 1947. It overhauled the way the Japanese ran their country and stripped the emperor of his power. His new role was to act as "the symbol of the State and of the unity of the People."[1] Japan's current flag, which was formally adopted on August 13, 1999, also exemplifies this mission.

The new constitution forced Japan to demilitarize, preventing the country from waging war. It expanded upon individual freedoms granted in the Meiji

Both the House of Representatives and the House of
Councillors meet at the National Diet Building in Tokyo.

Constitution, including freedom of speech and religion. The national government would be maintained through checks and balances between three branches of government—the legislative, executive, and judicial branches. Each branch contains separate agencies and employees.

On a local level, Japan was divided into prefectures. The country has 47 prefectures. Each has its own local government with a governor and representative assembly.

THE LEGISLATIVE BRANCH

The legislative branch in Japan is known as the *Kokkai*, or "Diet." It is the most influential body of power in the nation and makes the country's laws. The Diet is bicameral and is made of the House of Representatives and the House of Councillors. Members of both houses are elected by and represent the Japanese people. The number of Diet members is decided by electoral law and can vary between election years.

In 2021, the House of Representatives had 465 members.[2] Representatives serve four-year terms and must be at least

THE FLAG OF JAPAN

Since the Tokugawa shogunate fell and the Meiji government took control in 1868, Japan has flown the same national flag to represent the country. The flag consists of a red circle set against a white background. It is officially known as *Nisshoki*, which means "Flag of the Sun." It is also sometimes referred to as *Hinomaru*, or "Circle of the Sun."

25 years old to run for office. The House of Representatives is made of two subsets of representatives: single-seat constituencies and proportional-representation seats.

Japan is divided into voting districts. Each district is represented by a single-seat constituency representative. People vote to decide the single-seat constituency representative for their district. The person with the highest number of votes wins the seat for that district. The number of voting districts can vary each election. In the 2021 election, there were 289 single-seat constituencies.[3]

For proportional-representation seats, the country is divided into electoral blocs, which are larger than voting districts. Each bloc has a different number of proportional-representative seats, ranging from six to 26 seats. For proportional-representation seats, votes are cast for a party rather than an individual candidate. The number of seats a party receives is based on the number of votes it receives. In the 2021 election, there were 176 proportional-representation seats.[4]

After the 2019 elections, the House of Councillors had 245 members.[5] Each member serves for six years and must be at least 30 years old to run. Elections are staggered so that half of the

members are replaced or reelected every three years. Members of the House of Councillors represent the prefectures. Prefectures with larger populations have more councillors than those with smaller populations. In 2019, there were a total of 124 seats available in the House of Councillors. Seventy-four councillors were elected based on simple majorities in their prefectures. The remaining 50 seats were filled by proportional votes, in which people vote for a political party.[6] The entire country acts as a single voting district for proportional councillor seats.

In addition to creating laws, the Diet also approves treaties, elects a prime minister, and votes on the government's budget. Laws and legislative actions must be approved by both houses before they can go into effect. If the houses disagree, the Japanese Constitution declares that the House of Representatives has the higher authority. For example, if the House of Councillors rejects a bill that was passed by the House of Representatives, the House of Representatives can still get the law passed by resubmitting the bill to its chambers and winning a two-thirds majority vote.

THE EXECUTIVE BRANCH

The executive branch of government is made up of the prime minister and the cabinet. The Diet selects the prime minister, who then chooses cabinet members from the Diet. There is no limit to how long a prime minister can serve. In 2022, Shinzo Abe was the longest-serving prime minister in the country's history. He was prime minister from 2006 to 2007 and again from 2012 to 2020. Abe was fatally shot while giving a speech in July 2022.

The executive branch implements laws, engages in foreign diplomacy, and oversees public offices. The executive branch creates a budget and submits it to the Diet for approval. It also appoints the chief justice, signs peace agreements, and advises the emperor on the country's affairs.

THE JUDICIAL BRANCH

There are five types of courts in Japan: the Supreme Court, high courts, district courts, family courts, and summary courts. The Supreme Court is the highest court in the land. It consists of one chief justice and 14 associate judges, who are all appointed by the cabinet. Supreme Court judges serve for life and can be removed only by impeachment.

High courts sit directly below the Supreme Court. They rule on appeals of decisions made by lower courts. They are located in eight metropolitan areas: Tokyo, Osaka, Nagoya, Hiroshima, Fukuoka, Sendai, Sapporo, and Takamatsu.

District courts handle district-focused cases, such as criminal and civil cases. They are situated in

From 1954 to 2022, Japan has had 30 prime ministers. Only four of them—Kishi Nobusuke, Satō Eisaku, Nakasone Yasuhiro, and Shinzo Abe—served for more than two years.

50 locations nationwide—one in each of the 47 prefectures and one in Hakodate, Asahikawa, and Kushiro. Most district cases are presided over by a single judge.

Family courts and summary courts are the lowest courts. They hear domestic and juvenile cases, as well as lighter cases that may result in small fines. Similar to district cases, each of these family and summary courts is presided over by one judge.

In Japan, a case can be heard up to three times. The process begins in the lower court and can be bumped up to the high court. The Supreme Court is the final stop for a case. It determines the validity and constitutionality of all Japanese laws. Lower courts follow the rulings of higher courts, including the Supreme Court, when making decisions. The Supreme Court has the power to overturn a past Supreme Court ruling.

POLITICAL PARTIES

Japan has a multiparty system. Major parties include the Liberal Democratic Party (LDP), the Komeito, and the Constitutional Democratic Party of Japan (CDP). The LDP is the largest political party. It is a conservative party that supports bolstering Japan's military and preserving the country's economic growth. The LDP was founded in 1955. As of 2022, the LDP has been in power every year except from 1993 to 1994 and from 2009 to 2012. Since 1999, the LDP has had a coalition with Komeito, the center-right political faction of a Buddhist organization called Soka Gakkai. Komeito is also known as the Clean Government Party. Its aim is to promote world peace and uphold the rights of all human beings.

Emperor Hironomiya Naruhito delivered a speech at his enthronement ceremony in October 2019. Today, the emperor of Japan has only symbolic power.

The leading opposition party is the CDP. The CDP believes in strong national government, adherence to the constitution, a social security network, gender equality, and a pacifist outlook on global diplomacy. The party was formed in the run-up to the 2017 general election, when it merged with portions of the Democratic Party of the People.

A MIGHTY MILITARY

Japan's Self-Defense Force is one of the strongest militaries in the world. It was founded in 1954 after World War II. Today the Japanese military is ranked fifth globally behind the United States, Russia, China, and India in overall military power.[8]

In recent years, Japan has expanded military partnerships with Australia, Canada, the United Kingdom, France, and other European countries, as well as with the Association of Southeast Asian Nations. It spends tens of billions of dollars each year building up its military. As of 2021, it had nearly 1,000 warplanes.[9]

Some Japanese people support keeping the nation's military strong in case of attack. Others are cautious of military expansion. Japan is the only country to have been attacked with atomic bombs. Japanese people are worried that ramping up military spending could lead to similar tragedies.

Japan's Self-Defense Force distributed water to Japanese citizens after an earthquake in March 2022.

CHAPTER SEVEN

ECONOMICS

Japan has the third-largest economy in the world.[1] At the end of 2020, its gross domestic product (GDP) was about $5.04 trillion.[2] GDP is a way to measure the value of goods and services that a country produces within a certain period of time. A high GDP indicates a strong economy.

One of the reasons Japan has such a booming economy is because of its manufacturing industry and massive export market. The country's main exports are personal appliances, photo lab equipment, and transportation machinery. It exports most of its goods to China, the United States, and South Korea.

Japan is among the world's largest and most technologically advanced producers of motor vehicles and ships. It is a leading producer of

Fishing is a major industry in Japan. In 2019, there were more than 140,000 workers in this sector.

Sony is one of Japan's most popular brands. It makes cameras, televisions, electronics accessories, and video games.

manufacturing-related components such as steel, synthetic rubber, aluminum, sulfuric acid, plastics, cement, paper, and textiles. Japan also exports cameras and photography-related gear. Some of the most famous companies and brands are headquartered in Japan, including car companies such as Toyota, Honda, and Subaru and film and photography companies such as Sony, Canon, Fujifilm, and Panasonic.

Japanese manufacturing is concentrated in urban-industrial belts. These areas stretch outward from Tokyo along the Pacific coast and the Inland Sea to Kitakyushu in northern Kyushu. The largest manufacturing area is called the Keihin Industrial Zone. The zone covers Tokyo, Kawasaki, and Yokohama and is centered on the international ports in Tokyo Bay. Cars, computer parts, and other machinery are all made in the Keihin Industrial Zone. Other major manufacturing areas include Tōhoku, Shikoku, and Chūbu, which is where Toyota is headquartered.

VIDEO GAMES

The Japanese video game market is one of the largest and most influential in the world. The Nintendo Entertainment System, created by Japanese designer Masayuki Uemura, was released in 1983. Since then, the production of video games and related consoles has grown into a nearly $12.2 billion industry in the country.[3]

In 2021, the Nintendo Switch was the best-selling video game console in Japan.

Based in Kyoto, Nintendo is famous for its *Mario Bros.* franchise, which has sold more than 763 million copies since it was created in 1983.[5] Nintendo's prolific output includes other video game blockbusters such as *Donkey Kong*, *Pokémon*, and *The Legend of Zelda*. The company was also responsible for groundbreaking gaming consoles. The Game Boy became one of the first handheld gaming devices in the world when it was released in 1989. Nintendo released its first Wii console in 2006. Its motion-sensing and screen-pointing features made the console a huge success.

Japan is the headquarters for other video game companies. Sony created the original PlayStation in the mid-1990s. Since then, the company has released popular games such as *God of War* and *The Last of Us*. Square Enix, based in Tokyo, formed in 2003. It created the *Final Fantasy* video game series, one of the most widely distributed game series of all time.

INVENTIVE THINKING

Throughout history, Japan has been responsible for inventions that have changed the way society functions. In 1981, Japanese researchers at Honda came up with the world's first map-based car navigation system. Today, the country continues to push boundaries and come up with innovative and sustainable inventions.

Japan is making strides to change the way automobiles are produced. In 2009, Mitsubishi Motors announced it would be the first car manufacturing company in the world to mass-produce electric vehicles. Japan is considering a policy that would transition all vehicle manufacturing to hybrid electric by the mid-2030s, eliminating the need to produce vehicles that are powered by gasoline alone. In March 2020, there were 18,270 car-charging spots scattered around

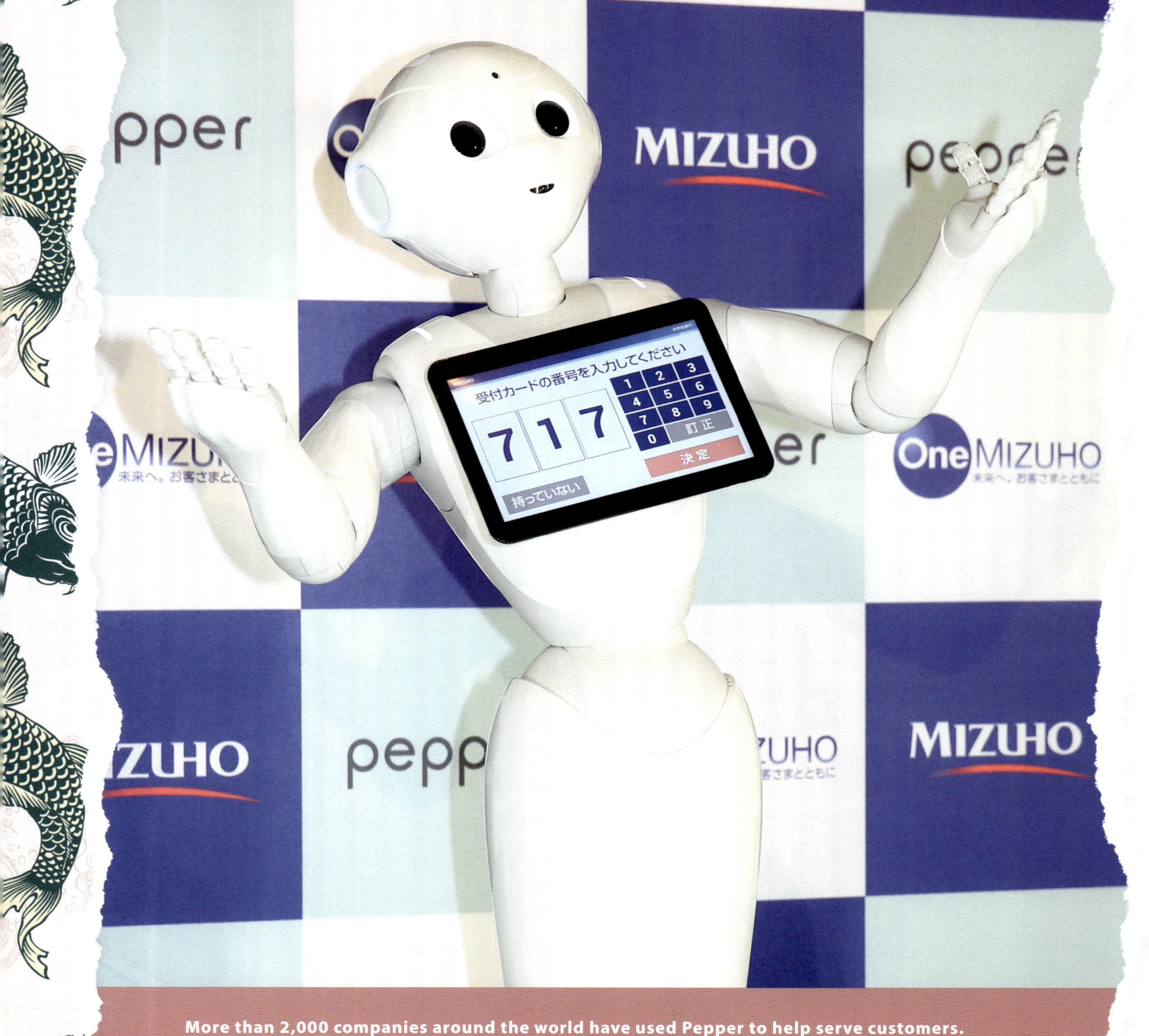

More than 2,000 companies around the world have used Pepper to help serve customers.

the country. The number of hybrid electric vehicles in Japan has also been increasing since 2014. By 2019, there were nearly 10.7 million hybrid vehicles being driven in the country.[6]

Since the 1970s, Japan has become a leader in the robotics industry. It manufactures robotic arms to assist in factories. It also makes remote-control devices that are programmed to enter dangerous areas, such as a crumbling building after an earthquake. In addition, Japan is a frontrunner in creating humanoid robots that are designed to help shoppers in stores, overworked parents at home, and elderly people in their daily lives. In 2015, SoftBank created a humanoid robot named Pepper. She could talk and recognize human emotions by analyzing people's facial expressions.

NUCLEAR POWER

Japan exports a lot of products. But it also relies on goods from other nations. Japan is poor in natural resources, such as natural gas and oil, so it relies heavily on other countries to supply these materials. Japan imports approximately 90 percent of its energy needs.[7] One of the country's main priorities is growing its nuclear energy use. Japan opened its first nuclear power plant in 1966. Through 2011, the country produced 30 percent of its energy from its nuclear reactors.[8]

On March 11, 2011, a 9.0-magnitude earthquake and tsunami decimated Japan's Pacific coast in the Fukushima prefecture. The nearby nuclear power plant was severely damaged. Many of its reactors were destroyed. Other reactors were shut down after public protests. Protesters called for the remaining reactors in the country to be dismantled until additional safety measures could

be put in place. Ten years after the disaster, Japan's nuclear power industry remains impaired but is slowly recovering. Two reactors went back online in 2015. By 2022, eight more had followed suit. Seventeen more are in the process of restarting. By 2030, the Japanese government hopes to be able to generate at least 20 percent of its energy from nuclear power.[9]

AGRICULTURE AND FISHING

Japan does not have enough farmable land to feed its large urban population. In fact, less than 4 percent of the Japanese workforce worked in agriculture in 2020.[10] The major products grown in Japan include rice, sweet potatoes, white potatoes, sugar beets, apples, mandarin oranges, and tea. However, the country imports about 60 percent of its food.[11]

In contrast, Japan has a thriving fishing economy because it is surrounded by water. The country has one of the largest fishing industries of any country in the world. There are more than 3,000 fishing ports scattered across the country.[12] These ports bring in all kinds of seafood,

An elderly woman harvests green tea in Shizuoka, Japan. In 2019, the average age for women working in agriculture was 67.6 years old.

including fish such as tuna, mackerel, and sardines, and other sea creatures, such as octopuses, crabs, and squid. In 2020, marine exports from Japan were valued at $2.2 billion.[14]

EMPLOYMENT NUMBERS

In 2021, Japan's workforce included 66.8 million people, which is approximately 60 percent of Japan's population.[15] For much of Japan's history, women have been at the margins of the workforce due to strict gender roles. For example, men were expected to work long hours and devote most of their lives to their companies, while women took care of most, if not all, of the housework and child-rearing. However, this attitude is shifting, and more women have entered the workforce in recent years.

In 2013, prime minister Shinzo Abe set a goal to create "a society where women can shine."[16] In 2019, 44.5 percent of the total workforce in Japan was female.[17] Still, some scholars are skeptical that women are benefiting enough from the change.

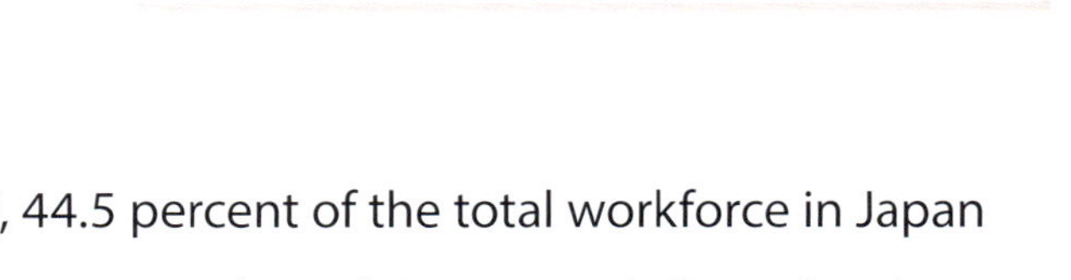

Sushi chef and manager Yuki Chidui prepares sushi at her all-female restaurant. Making sushi was historically seen as a male tradition in Japan.

Men make up the majority of senior positions in Japan. A 2017 Japanese government report found that women made up only 13 percent of managerial positions in Japan, compared with 44 percent in the United States.[18] Women are also still expected to do the majority of the housework and childcare on top of their jobs. The World Economic Forum's *Global Gender Gap Report 2021* ranked Japan 120th out of 156 countries in terms of gender equality.[19] Critics insist that even though more

Japan's bullet trains can travel up to 199 miles per hour (320 kmh).

Japanese women are working today than in the past, the country still has a long way to go in order to make the workplace an equitable place to be.

TRANSPORTATION NETWORK

Japan is a well-connected country. Its sprawling cities and countryside are serviced by an extensive network of railways, roads, airplane routes, and sea channels. The major islands are connected through a series of well-maintained bridges and undersea tunnels. Most families in Japan own at least one car. Roadways are congested since trucks transport products all over the country.

For faster travel, the Shinkansen is considered one of the speediest and safest rail systems in the world. The trains feature comfortable, cushioned seats in regular-fare and business-class cars. There are bathrooms on board and electrical outlets at each seat. Food and beverage service is provided. Aside from the bullet train, Japan has a passenger railway network, subway systems in its major cities, and a ferry system that takes passengers between the country's islands.

Domestic air service links dozens of airports in major cities. Japan Airlines and All Nippon Airways are the two major international carriers. They operate out of four international airports in Japan and fly to destinations around the world.

CHAPTER EIGHT

JAPAN TODAY

Today, Japan is a prosperous and fascinating country. It abounds with festivals, museums, and sacred spaces. Its technological innovations in health-related fields, elder care, and vehicle efficiency are paving the way for progress in the world. Yet despite its status as one of the world's leading superpowers, Japan has faced some setbacks in the last few decades. On January 3, 2020, the country was hit with its first case of COVID-19.[1] From January 2020 to June 2022, there were more than 9.2 million confirmed cases in Japan, according to the World Health Organization.[2] More than 31,000 Japanese people had died from the illness by June 27, 2022.[3] Through that same time, more than 280 million doses of COVID-19 vaccines had been administered.[4]

A major historical landmark in Japan is the Great Buddha statue of Kamakura, which was built starting in 1252.

The COVID-19 pandemic affected Japan in many ways. Schools and businesses closed to prevent students and workers from getting sick. Students had to attend school virtually, and many workers who were able to shifted to remote work. These measures protected public health but hurt the economy. Unemployment numbers rose as industries struggled. Closures led to supply chain disruptions. The worldwide shutdown caused the Japanese economy to drop 29 percent. Exports dropped by 11 percent, their lowest point since 2012. In December 2020, wages fell for the tenth month in a row, falling to their worst level since 2014.[5] However, COVID-19 did not affect the Japanese economy as much as the economies of the United States and European countries.

International and domestic tourism in the country screeched to a halt too. The Tokyo Summer Olympic Games were supposed to be held in 2020, but they were postponed due to the pandemic. When the Games were rescheduled for the summer of 2021, no foreign spectators were allowed to attend in person. Japanese nationals could go, but crowds would be limited to a maximum of 10,000 people.

The COVID-19 pandemic hurt Japan's economy, but the country is slowly on the mend. As businesses and schools reopen, daily life in Japan is beginning to return to pre-pandemic levels. Japanese people are returning to work and enjoying outings with their families.

The Japanese government released health guidelines during the COVID-19 pandemic that included wearing a face mask.

Until her death in 2022, Japanese citizen Kane Tanaka was the oldest living person in the world at 119 years old.

WORK-LIFE BALANCE

Japan has universal health insurance, and any Japanese person can get the medical treatments or prescription drugs they need. The system is financed through taxes and individual payments into the program. It can be accessed through a mandatory employer health insurance policy. It can also be accessed through a residence-based program, which includes medical insurance for the elderly.

Thanks in part to its universal health care system and a nutritious traditional diet of fish and rice, Japan has one of the highest life expectancies in the world. In 2022, the average life expectancy was 87.9 years for women and 81.9 years for men.[7] That's the fourth-highest ranking in the world behind Monaco, Singapore, and Macau.[8]

But the country struggles with attitudes about mental health. One major concern is the work-life balance—or lack thereof—in the country. Especially in urban centers where the top manufacturing, financial, and business firms are located, the Japanese office environment is known for long hours and heavy workloads. Though many companies give 20 days off per year to their employees, some employees don't take much time off because they feel the need to provide for their families or don't want to look bad in the eyes of

their bosses. Other employees are rarely absent because they don't want to burden their coworkers with more work. In 2018, workers took only 52.4 percent of the paid leave they were given.[9]

This pressure to succeed in the workplace can lead to stressful interactions at home or heavy drinking at business-related outings. In the most extreme cases, Japanese workers have taken their own lives because they couldn't deal with the anxiety. In 2021, 1,935 people in Japan lost their lives to suicide as a result of work-related stress.[10]

For many Japanese people, working their way up the corporate ladder can seem like an all-encompassing goal. But in 2018, the Japanese government intervened to try to come up with a solution to the problem. Initiated by prime minister Shinzo Abe, the Diet passed the Work Style Reform Bill. It amended eight key labor laws and provided incentives for people to take more of a balanced approach to work. Some of the incentives included limits on work hours and a requirement that employers had to mandate at least five days off per year for staff who hadn't used ten days of their vacation time. Today, there are signs that the younger generations are taking strides to achieve a healthier work-life balance in the future.

FAMILY FULFILLMENT

Beyond working, family—referred to as *kazoku*—is considered a top priority in Japan and the foundation of a fulfilling existence. Many households are multigenerational, with the husband at the head and one or both sets of grandparents living under the same roof. While today both men and women work, the gender roles in Japan have historically had the husband responsible for bringing home a majority of the money and the wife as the primary caregiver. Today, the wife is still expected to manage the children, clean the house, keep track of the family budget, and plan the social calendar in addition to any lower-paying or part-time work.

Eighty-five percent of single mothers in Japan are part of the workforce.[11]

Mothers are typically responsible for enrolling their children in primary and secondary education. The structure of the education system in Japan is much like it is in the United States. Children move through elementary, junior high, and senior high school, followed by higher education at a college or university. Japanese children are required to go to school for nine years total—six years of elementary school and three years of lower secondary education. Anything after that is up to the parents and the student. In 2020, nearly all

With more than 28,000 students, the University of Tokyo is one of the largest universities in Japan.

children in Japan attended school until the ninth grade. About 59 percent of Japanese kids were enrolled in a university or technical college.[12]

Outside of the family structure, dating in Japan involves many traditions. One popular practice is called *gokon*, which can be compared to a group blind date. The name stems from the Japanese words *godo*, which means "mixed" or "combination," and *konpa*, which means "informal group meeting." One couple or individual invites their single male and female friends out to a restaurant or bar. At first the men and women sit across from each other. Over the course of the evening, they move around according to whom they think they might click with best. The goal is to find a suitable romantic partner.

Like in many countries around the world, same-sex marriage was illegal in Japan until recently. Article 24 of its constitution defines marriage as based on the "mutual consent of both sexes," which had historically been interpreted to mean between a man and woman.[13] However, the marriage restrictions seem to be changing. In a groundbreaking case in March 2021, the Sapporo District Court ruled that the government's ban on gay marriage was unconstitutional. Later that same year, a court in Tokyo followed suit. It decided that same-sex marriage would be legal in the country's capital beginning in April 2022.

A CONSIDERATE CULTURE

Japanese people have developed a reputation for being polite and showing considerate behavior. Etiquette is practiced and strictly followed throughout the country. For example, being punctual

A traditional Japanese tea ceremony has many etiquette rules, including removing one's shoes and entering the room on one's knees.

is key. Lateness implies disrespect for another person's time. Cleanliness is also important. Japanese people remove their shoes before entering someone's home. Some restaurants with special flooring may ask customers to remove their shoes. Special shoes are worn inside. Some eating establishments or homes also have separate slippers that are worn inside the bathroom.

At stores, it is considered impolite to hand money directly to a cashier. Instead, there is a small dish next to the cash register. Customers place their bills or coins in the dish so the clerk can retrieve the cash.

There are also many unspoken rules about dining in Japan. Certain behaviors are considered respectful while others are seen as rude. Blowing one's nose at the dinner table is frowned upon, but slurping is seen as a sign of approval for the chef. It is not considered rude to leave food on the plate, but serving guests too much food is seen as impolite. Tipping, while appreciated in some cultures, isn't usually practiced in Japan.

Japan has some of the most celebrated World Heritage sites, including the historic Himeji Castle. The castle complex is one of the best preserved castles in Japan.

Omotenashi, which translates to "hospitality," is the concept that informs etiquette in Japan. It means being thoughtful and mindful of others. This can extend to wearing a mask on a bus to prevent other passengers from getting sick or to the way a guest should be treated when visiting a home. In general, the honor for a host lies in anticipating the needs of their guests, not in doing a good deed so the favor can one day be returned.

A BOUNTIFUL COUNTRY

There is a reason that more than 32 million tourists visit Japan annually.[14] It is a prosperous nation full of busy cities and peaceful seaside villages, magnificent flora and fauna, and sacred spaces that calm the soul. In the coming years, the government hopes to reach a milestone of 40 million visitors annually.

Travel experts agree the goal is highly possible. In fact, just a year before the COVID-19 pandemic swept the globe, *Travel + Leisure* magazine named Japan the 2018 Destination of the Year. "It practically goes without saying that the rich, cultural history and delicious food are the key reasons why people want to visit this special country in the first place. . . . Japan's gorgeous cherry blossoms and festivals are occasions everyone simply must see in their lifetime," reporter Andrea Romano wrote. "As you're making travel plans for the year ahead, be sure to add Japan to your list, whether you've already been there or not. There's always more to see."[15]

OFFICIAL NAME: JAPAN

GEOGRAPHY

Area: 145,914 square miles (377,915 sq km)

Highest Elevation: Mount Fuji at 12,388 feet (3,776 m)

Lowest Elevation: Hachirō Lagoon at −13 feet (−4 m)

PEOPLE

Population: 124.2 million (2022 est.)

Most Populous City: Tokyo (37 million)

Ethnic Groups: Mostly Japanese, also Chinese, Korean, other

Religions: Shinto, Buddhism, Christianity, other

GOVERNMENT

Type of Government: Parliamentary constitutional monarchy

Capital: Tokyo

Head of State: Emperor

Head of Government: Prime minister

Legislature: Bicameral, with a House of Representatives and a House of Councillors that together form the Diet

ECONOMY

Currency: Japanese yen

Major Industries: Motor vehicles, electronic equipment, machine tools, ships, chemicals

Natural Resources: Fish, extremely limited mineral and energy resources

NATIONAL SYMBOLS

National Anthem: "Kimigayo" ("The Emperor's Reign")

National Bird: Green pheasant

National Flower: Chrysanthemum

GLOSSARY

ARCHIPELAGO

A group of islands, or a stretch of sea containing many islands.

BICAMERAL

Having two legislative chambers.

CONSTITUENCY

A body of voters in a specific designated area who elect a representative to a legislative body.

DYNASTY

A succession of rulers in the same family line.

GEISHA

A Japanese girl or woman who is trained to provide conversation, dancing, singing, or other entertainment, especially for a man or a group of men.

INNOVATIVE

Having original new methods and features.

METROPOLITAN

Relating to an area that includes a large city and its surrounding suburbs.

PERENNIAL

Capable of producing new blooms or growth for multiple years.

PROLIFIC

Producing many works.

SECULAR

Nonreligious.

SEISMIC

Relating to the shaking of the surface of Earth.

SOVEREIGN

Possessing ultimate power.

TECTONIC

Relating to the structure of Earth's crust and the processes that take place within it, including shifting and earthquakes.

TRANSCEND

To go beyond the universe or ordinary existence.

ADDITIONAL RESOURCES

SELECTED BIBLIOGRAPHY

"Japan." *CIA World Factbook*, 30 Mar. 2022, cia.gov. Accessed 23 May 2022.

Japan Wildlife Research Center. *The Wildlife in Japan.* Ministry of the Environment, 2015.

"Japanese Culture." *Cultural Atlas*, 2022, culturalatlas.sbs.com.au. Accessed 23 May 2022.

FURTHER READINGS

DK Eyewitness Japan. DK Eyewitness Travel, 2019.

García, Héctor. *A Geek in Japan: Discovering the Land of Manga, Anime, Zen, and the Tea Ceremony.* Tuttle, 2019.

Marcovitz, Hal. *Cause & Effect: World War II.* ReferencePoint, 2018.

ONLINE RESOURCES

To learn more about Japan, please visit **abdobooklinks.com** or scan this QR code. These links are routinely monitored and updated to provide the most current information available.

MORE INFORMATION

For more information on this subject, contact or visit the following organizations:

Embassy of Japan in the United States of America

2520 Massachusetts Ave. NW

Washington, DC 20008

us.emb-japan.go.jp/itprtop_en/index.html

The Embassy of Japan in the United States provides assistance to Japanese citizens who are traveling or planning to travel to the United States. It answers questions and protects Japanese citizens who are abroad.

Tokyo National Museum

13-9 Uenokoen

Taito City, Tokyo 110-8712, Japan

tnm.jp

The Tokyo National Museum displays artwork such as photographs and fine art from Japan and other Asian countries. It is dedicated to the preservation of Asian cultures and has been in operation for more than 150 years.

SOURCE NOTES

CHAPTER 1. A TOUR OF JAPAN
1. "Shinkansen." *Japan-Guide.com*, 25 June 2022, japan-guide.com. Accessed 27 June 2022.
2. "Highest Point: 634 m." *Tokyo Skytree*, n.d., tokyo-skytree.jp. Accessed 27 June 2022.
3. "Fushimi Inari Taisha." *Fushimi Inari Taisha*, n.d., inari.jp. Accessed 27 June 2022.
4. "Fushimi Inari Taisha." *Japan-Guide.com*, 11 Aug. 2020, japan-guide.com. Accessed 27 June 2022.
5. "Fushimi Inari Taisha Shrine." *Japan*, n.d., japan.travel. Accessed 27 June 2022.
6. John Asano. "A Brief History of Osaka Castle." *Culture Trip*, 10 Apr. 2017, theculturetrip.com. Accessed 27 June 2022.
7. Amancay Tapia. "The 25 Most Populous Cities in the World." *Newsweek*, 3 Oct. 2021, newsweek.com. Accessed 27 June 2022.
8. "Takachiho Gorge." *Visit Kyushu*, 2022, visit-kyushu.com. Accessed 27 June 2022.

CHAPTER 2. GEOGRAPHY
1. "Japan: A Geographical Sketch." *Asian Art Outlook*, 2022, sites.asiasociety.org. Accessed 27 June 2022.
2. "Statistical Handbook of Japan 2021." *Statistics Bureau of Japan*, 2021, stat.go.jp. Accessed 27 June 2022.
3. "Japan: A Nation of Nearly 7,000 Islands." *Nippon.com*, 11 Sept. 2020, nippon.com. Accessed 27 June 2022.
4. "Japan: A Nation of Nearly 7,000 Islands," *Nippon.com*.
5. Aaron Spray. "Okinawa: Visiting Japan's 'Fifth' Major Island Paradise." *Travel*, 24 Jan. 2022, thetravel.com. Accessed 27 June 2022.
6. "Iwo Jima and Okinawa: Death at Japan's Doorstep." *National WWII Museum*, n.d., nationalww2museum.org. Accessed 27 June 2022.
7. "Ring of Fire." *National Geographic*, 20 May 2022, education.nationalgeographic.org. Accessed 27 June 2022.
8. Eisuke Fujita, Hideki Ueda, and Setsuya Nakada. "A New Japan Volcanological Database." *Frontiers in Earth Science*, 10 July 2020, frontiersin.org. Accessed 27 June 2022.
9. "Mount Fuji." *Encyclopedia Britannica*, 26 Aug. 2021, britannica.com. Accessed 27 June 2022.
10. "Statistical Handbook of Japan 2021," *Statistics Bureau of Japan*.
11. "What Are the Key Facts of Japan?" *Maps of World*, 5 Sept. 2020, mapsofworld.com. Accessed 27 June 2022.
12. Franz Lidz. "Why Mount Fuji Endures as a Powerful Force in Japan." *Smithsonian Magazine*, May 2017, smithsonianmag.com. Accessed 27 June 2022.
13. Lidz, "Why Mount Fuji Endures as a Powerful Force in Japan," *Smithsonian Magazine*.
14. "Kitayamazaki Cliffs." *Iwate Prefecture*, 2018, visitiwate.com. Accessed 27 June 2022.
15. Benjamin Elisha Sawe. "The Longest Rivers in Japan." *World Atlas*, 21 Aug. 2019, worldatlas.com. Accessed 27 June 2022.
16. "Climate and Monthly Weather Forecast Japan." *Weather Atlas*, n.d., weather-atlas.com. Accessed 27 June 2022.
17. Michael Case and Andrea Tidwell. "Nippon Changes." *World Wildlife Foundation*, n.d., wwf.or.jp. Accessed 27 June 2022.
18. "What Are the Key Facts of Japan?" *Maps of World*.
19. "Climate and Monthly Weather Forecast Japan," *Weather Atlas*.
20. "Climate and Monthly Weather Forecast Japan," *Weather Atlas*.
21. "Landslide and Disaster Preparedness in Japan." *Prevention Web*, 8 July 2021, preventionweb.net. Accessed 27 June 2022.

CHAPTER 3. PLANTS AND ANIMALS

1. "Japan - Main Details." *Convention on Biological Diversity*, 2022, cbd.int. Accessed 27 June 2022.
2. "Japan - Main Details," *Convention on Biological Diversity*.
3. "Japan - Main Details," *Convention on Biological Diversity*.
4. "Japan - Main Details," *Convention on Biological Diversity*.
5. "Japanese Golden Eagle." *Yamaha*, n.d., global.yamaha-motor.com. Accessed 27 June 2022.
6. Jon Heggie. "Japan: Saving Species in One of the World's Biodiversity Hotspots." *National Geographic*, 3 Dec. 2021, nationalgeographic.co.uk. Accessed 27 June 2022.
7. "Japan: Red List Category." *IUCN Red List of Threatened Species*, 2021, iucnredlist.org. Accessed 27 June 2022.
8. "Humpback Whale." *Encyclopedia Britannica*, 22 Nov. 2019, britannica.com. Accessed 27 June 2022.
9. "Ogasawara Islands." *UNESCO*, 2022, whc.unesco.org. Accessed 27 June 2022.
10. "Ogasawara Islands." *World Heritage Datasheet*, Jan. 2012, world-heritage-datasheets.unep-wcmc.org. Accessed 27 June 2022.
11. "Jomon Sugi." *Japan*, n.d., japan.travel. Accessed 27 June 2022.

CHAPTER 4. HISTORY

1. "Japan's Encounter with Europe, 1573–1853." *Victoria and Albert Museum*, 2022, vam.ac.uk. Accessed 27 June 2022.
2. "A Timeline of Christianity in Japan." *Nippon.com*, 25 Nov. 2019, nippon.com. Accessed 27 June 2022.
3. Yvette Tan. "The Japanese Christians Forced to Trample on Christ." *BBC*, 24 Nov. 2019, bbc.com. Accessed 27 June 2022.
4. Erin Blakemore. "How Japan Took Control of Korea." *History*, 28 July 2020, history.com. Accessed 27 June 2022.
5. "Sino-Japanese War." *History*, 2022, history.co.uk. Accessed 27 June 2022.
6. Rob Citno. "Pearl Harbor Attack, December 7, 1941." *National WWII Museum*, 2022, nationalww2museum.org. Accessed 27 June 2022.
7. "The Atomic Bombings of Hiroshima and Nagasaki." *Atomicarchive.com*, 2020, atomicarchive.com. Accessed 27 June 2022.

CHAPTER 5. PEOPLE AND CULTURE

1. "Japan Population 2022 (Live)." *World Population Review*, 2022, worldpopulationreview.com. Accessed 27 June 2022.
2. "Japan's Ageing Society." *European Parliament*, Dec. 2020, europarl.europa.eu. Accessed 27 June 2022.
3. "Statistical Handbook of Japan 2021." *Statistics Bureau of Japan*, 2021, stat.go.jp. Accessed 27 June 2022.
4. "Japan's Ageing Society," *European Parliament*.
5. "Statistical Handbook of Japan 2021," *Statistics Bureau of Japan*.
6. "Japan." *CIA World Factbook*, 21 June 2022, cia.gov. Accessed 27 June 2022.
7. "Tokyo, Japan Metro Area Population 1950–2022." *Macrotrends*, 2022, macrotrends.net. Accessed 27 June 2022.
8. "2020 Report on International Religious Freedom: Japan." *US Department of State*, 21 May 2021, state.gov. Accessed 27 June 2022.
9. Mark Cartwright. "Shinto." *World History Encyclopedia*, 3 Apr. 2017, worldhistory.org. Accessed 27 June 2022.
10. "2020 Report on International Religious Freedom," *US Department of State*.
11. "Manga Industry in Japan - Statistics and Facts." *Statista*, 31 Jan. 2022, statista.com. Accessed 27 June 2022.
12. John Spacey. "Kaiseki: The Japanese Art of Food." *Japan Talk*, 19 Jan. 2014, japan-talk.com. Accessed 27 June 2022.

CHAPTER 6. POLITICS

1. Amy Gunia. "Five Things to Know about the Modern Japanese Monarchy." *Time*, 29 Apr. 2019, time.com. Accessed 27 June 2022.

2. "Japan." *ElectionGuide*, 31 Oct. 2021, electionguide.org. Accessed 27 June 2022.

3. "Japan," *ElectionGuide*.

4. "Japan," *ElectionGuide*.

5. "Japan," *ElectionGuide*, 21 July 2019, electionguide.org. Accessed 27 June 2022.

6. "Japan," *ElectionGuide*. 21 July 2019.

7. "Rate of Women Holding Leadership Positions in Politics in Japan from Fiscal Year 2016 to 2021, by Type of Politician." *Statista*, 24 May 2022, statista.com. Accessed 27 June 2022.

8. Mari Yamaguchi. "Japan's Military, among World's Strongest, Looks to Build." *ABC News*, 6 Dec. 2021, abcnews.go.com. Accessed 27 June 2022.

9. Yamaguchi, "Japan's Military," *ABC News*.

CHAPTER 7. ECONOMICS

1. "Japan." *OEC*, Mar. 2022, oec.world. Accessed 27 June 2022.

2. Aaron O'Neill. "Japan: Gross Domestic Product (GDP) in Current Prices from 1987 to 2027." *Statista*, 18 May 2022, statista.com. Accessed 27 June 2022.

3. "Total Value of the Video Game Market in Japan in Fiscal Year 2020 with a Forecast until 2027." *Statista*, 1 Feb. 2022, statista.com. Accessed 27 June 2022.

4. "Japan," *OEC*.

5. Garrett Martin. "The 10 Best-Selling Nintendo Franchises of All Time." *Paste*, 18 Apr. 2022, pastemagazine.com. Accessed 27 June 2022.

6. "Manufacturing." *JETRO*, Mar. 2021, jetro.go.jp. Accessed 27 June 2022.

7. "Nuclear Power in Japan." *World Nuclear Association*, June 2022, world-nuclear.org. Accessed 27 June 2022.

8. "Nuclear Power in Japan," *World Nuclear Association*.

9. "Japan Backs Role of Nuclear Power in 2030 Energy Plan." *Reuters*, 16 May 2018, reuters.com. Accessed 27 June 2022.

10. "2022 Global Workforce Trends." *Trading Economics*, 2022, tradingeconomics.com. Accessed 27 June 2022.

11. Thisanka Siripala. "Japan's Weak Yen Hampers Its Post-COVID Recovery." *Diplomat*, 12 May 2022, thediplomat.com. Accessed 27 June 2022.

12. Mitsuharu Kume. "The Japanese Fisherman: An Endangered Species." *Outdoor Japan*, May 2010, outdoorjapan.com. Accessed 27 June 2022.

13. "Fukushima Disaster: What Happened at the Nuclear Plant?" *BBC*, 10 Mar. 2021, bbc.com. Accessed 27 June 2022.

14. "Export Value of Commodities from the Fisheries and Aquaculture Industry from Japan from 2012 to 2021." *Statista*, 3 June 2022, statista.com. Accessed 27 June 2022.

15. "Employment Rate in Japan from 1973 to 2021." *Statista*, 23 Feb. 2022, statista.com. Accessed 27 June 2022.

16. Brook Larmer. "Why Does Japan Make It So Hard for Working Women to Succeed?" *New York Times*, 17 Oct. 2018, nytimes.com. Accessed 27 June 2022.

17. Daichi Mishima. "Japan Sees Record Number of Women Working, but Challenges Remain." *Nikkei Asia*, 30 July 2019, asia.nikkei.com. Accessed 27 June 2022.

18. Larmer, "Why Does Japan Make It So Hard for Working Women to Succeed?"

19. Mariko Oi. "Why Japan Can't Shake Sexism." *BBC*, 8 Apr. 2021, bbc.com. Accessed 27 June 2022.

20. "Japan Economic and Trade Fact Sheet." *Australian Government*, 2020, dfat.gov.au. Accessed 27 June 2022.

CHAPTER 8. JAPAN TODAY

1. "Japan." *World Health Organization*, 27 June 2022, covid19.who.in. Accessed 27 June 2022.

2. "Japan," *World Health Organization*.

3. "Japan," *World Health Organization*.

4. "Japan," *World Health Organization*.

5. Paul Nadeau. "Revisiting the Economic Impact of COVID-19 on Japan." *Tokyo Review*, 10 Sept. 2021, tokyoreview.net. Accessed 27 June 2022.

6. Noriko Yagasaki. "Impact of COVID-19 on the Japanese Travel Market and the Travel Market of Overseas Visitors to Japan, and Subsequent Recovery." *IATSS Research*, Dec. 2021, sciencedirect.com. Accessed 27 June 2022.

7. "Japan." *CIA World Factbook*, 21 June 2022, cia.gov. Accessed 27 June 2022.

8. "Japan," *CIA World Factbook*.

9. Danielle Demetriou. "How the Japanese Are Putting an End to Extreme Work Weeks." *BBC*, 17 Jan. 2020, bbc.com. Accessed 27 June 2022.

10. L. Kettenhofen. "Number of Suicides Related to Problems at Work in Japan from 2012 to 2021." *Statista*, 5 Apr. 2022, statista.com. Accessed 27 June 2022.

11. Alana Semuels. "Japan Is No Place for Single Mothers." *Atlantic*, 7 Sept. 2017, theatlantic.com. Accessed 27 June 2022.

12. "Enrollment Rate at Universities and Junior Colleges in Japan from Fiscal Year 1960 to 2020, by Gender." *Statista*, 1 Mar. 2022, statista.com. Accessed 27 June 2022.

13. Rachel Treisman. "In Landmark Ruling, Court Says Japan's Ban on Same-Sex Marriage Is Unconstitutional." *NPR*, 17 Mar. 2021, npr.org. Accessed 27 June 2022.

14. Alexandru Arba. "Number of International Visitors to Japan from 2005 to 2021." *Statista*, 6 May 2022, statista.com. Accessed 27 June 2022.

15. Andrea Romano. "Why Japan Is Travel + Leisure's 2018 Destination of the Year (Video)." *Travel + Leisure*, 14 Nov. 2018, travelandleisure.com. Accessed 27 June 2022.

ABOUT THE **AUTHOR**

ALEXIS BURLING

Alexis Burling has written dozens of articles and books for young readers on a variety of topics, including current events, biographies, nutrition and fitness, careers, and money management. She is also a professional book critic who has written reviews of adult and young adult books, author interviews, and other publishing industry–related articles for the *New York Times*, the *Washington Post Book World*, the *San Francisco Chronicle*, and more. Burling has had the pleasure of visiting Japan in 2016, and she can't wait to go back. In fact, many of Suki's experiences were the path Burling followed on her own journey. Burling lives in White Salmon, Washington, with her husband and cats.